CAMERA CRAFTS

creative projects to make with your
camera and a good roll of film

BY
CYNDI FINKLE
ILLUSTRATED BY JUDY MACDONALD

LOWELL HOUSE JUVENILE

LOS ANGELES

CONTEMPORY BOOKS

CHICAGO

To Temple W. Williams III who is my love, my life,
my husband, and my inspiration.

—C. F.

Publisher: Jack Artenstein
Director of Publishing Services: Rena Copperman
Managing Editor, Juvenile Division: Lindsey Hay
Editor in Chief, Juvenile Division, Nonfiction: Amy Downing
Art Director: Lisa-Theresa Lenthall
Typesetting: Justin Segal
Cover photographs: Cyndi Finkle
Cover crafts: Charlene Olexiewicz

Library of Congress Catalog Card Number is available.

ISBN: 1-56565-706-3

Lowell House books can be purchased at special discounts when ordered in bulk for
premiums and special sales.
Contact Department TC at the following address:

Lowell House Juvenile
2020 Avenue of the Stars, Suite 300
Los Angeles, CA 90067

Manufactured in the United States of America
10 9 8 7 6 5 4 3 2

Contents

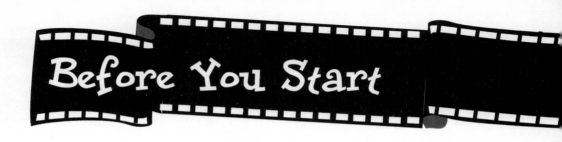

Before You Start

Photography is a wonderful art form because it combines ideas, technique, skill, and inspiration, resulting in a photograph that is everlasting and can be reproduced.

There are many types of photography, including nature, sports, travel, scenic, documentary, art, portrait, and special effects. As you take more and more pictures, you will decide what is your favorite type of photography.

A 35mm camera is the most popular, convenient, and versatile of all the kinds available. You can use a fully automatic (point and shoot) camera, a semiautomatic (both manual and automatic), or a fully manual camera.

I recommend the semiautomatic for the crafts in this book because you need to have the option of specific settings for such projects as the self-portraits and ghost writing. However, you can use the automatic settings for most of the other crafts.

Have fun with photography. Use it to document, express yourself, make memories, and be creative. The possibilities are endless and the results inspiring.

Enjoy the projects and have fun making personal gifts for your family and friends!

Cheers.

Cyndi Finkle

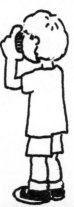

Personalized Book Cover

Using photographs and miscellaneous cutouts, make your own book cover using a glue that seals on the images and creates a long-lasting book.

MATERIALS

- newspaper
- photographs of family, friends, and pets
- notebook or journal with a plain cover (5" x 7" black sketch books with blank pages work best for this)
- paintbrush
- Mod Podge™ (or other water based sealer, glue, and finish)

PHOTO PREP!

Decide what you want on your book cover. You can put one picture on the book or a mixture of photos and cutouts from magazines. Use the book as a journal (choose pictures of yourself), a sketch book (choose pictures of your favorite artist's work), or as a phone book and message pad (choose pictures of your friends and family).

WHAT TO DO

1 Clear a work area and cover it with newspaper. Arrange your photos and cutouts on the book.

2 Using your paintbrush, affix the photos with the Mod Podge. Mod Podge will attach the photos to the book and seal them permanently. Let it dry. (If you do get any on your hands or clothes, wash it off with soap and water.)

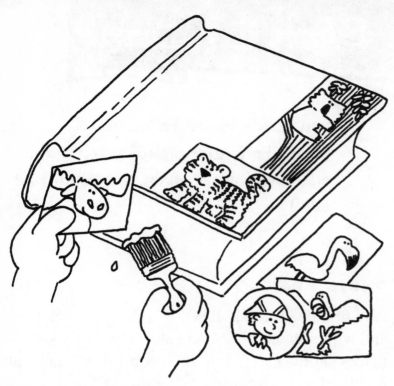

3 Brush another coat of Mod Podge over the entire front of the book. If you are also putting pictures on the back, first let the front dry completely. The glue will turn sort of white while it is drying, but it will dry clear. Now your cover will be sturdy enough to protect the book for years to come.

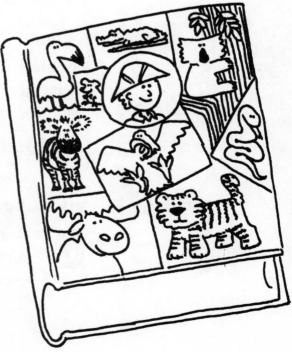

Photos from Back in Time

You don't have to be an old-timer to create photos with an old-fashioned flair. It's all in the film!

MATERIALS

- ILFORD XPII film
- any 35mm camera
- old clothes or costumes
- neat old objects such as books, boots, or dolls
- old-fashioned silver frame

PHOTO PREP!

You first need to buy ILFORD XPII film, a black-and-white film. Most camera stores or film supply places should carry this. You probably will not find it at the local drugstore or supermarket.

What you will have is a black-and-white negative, but if you request the lab to run it through their color printing machines, the prints will come out brown toned and old-fashioned looking.

WHAT TO DO

 1. You can take still-life pictures of objects such as books, dolls, car or plane models, or jewelry.

Or, have your family dress up in old-style clothing and take pictures of them, using the ILFORD XPII film.

 Take the roll of film to any color processing place. Tell the lab that you want color prints made. They will process the film for you using C-41, a color process for black-and-white film.

    For this type of prints you really need to emphasize to the lab what you are trying to achieve. Since most color labs do not deal with black-and-white film, once they process it, they will often send it out to a black-and-white lab for prints. This means they will give you normal black-and-white prints, which are usually expensive and will not have the brown tint.

To avoid a mistake by the lab, include the following instructions:

Dear Photo Lab:

I shot my pictures with ILFORD XPII film because I want color prints made that have a brownish and old-fashioned look.
    Please:

1) Process the film in C-41.

2) Make machine prints by using the ILFORD negative in the color print machine.

I do not want black-and-white prints made from these negatives.

9

*In advance, thank you for your attention to
this special order.*

 When you pick up your photos, you can choose your favorite and put it
into an old-fashioned silver frame.

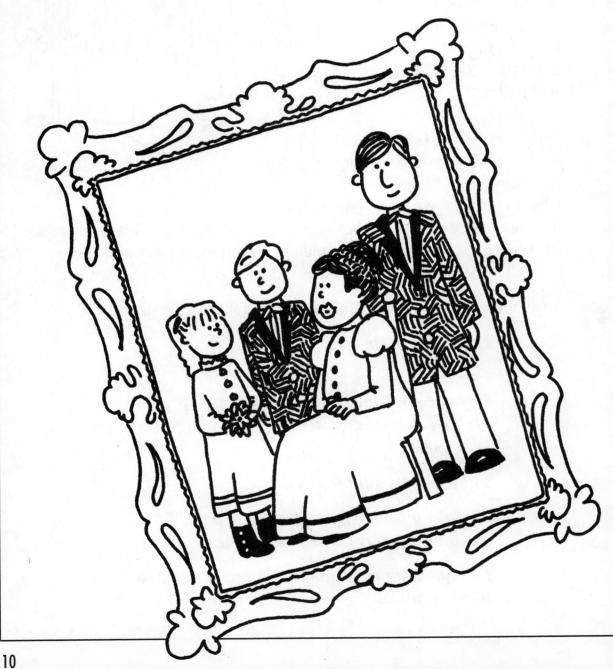

Personal Photo Calendar

Remember friends and family throughout the year by creating this personalized monthly calendar.

MATERIALS

- thirteen 5" x 7" photographs
- seven sheets of 11" x 17" construction paper
- hole punch
- string or twine
- colored markers
- ruler
- calendar for upcoming year
- glue

PHOTO PREP!

Choose 12 photos that you want to include in your calendar and 1 photo for the cover. Pick photos that represent the different months. For example, choose your favorite winter holiday photo for December, and make sure you pick a photograph of yourself for the month in which you were born. If you can't use 5" x 7" photos, you can better fill your calendar by using two 3½" x 5" prints for each month.

WHAT TO DO

 Fold each sheet of construction paper in half. Stack them on top of each other. This will give you 12 months, a cover, and a page at the back to record phone numbers or write a personal note if you are making the calendar for someone else.

2 Punch three evenly spaced holes along the folds using the hole punch. Thread a small piece of twine or string through the center hole and tie it into a bow. Repeat with the two outside holes. You want to be able to open and shut the calendar with ease, so don't tie the strings too tight.

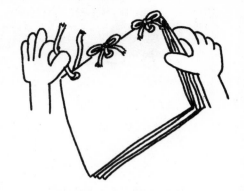

3 When the calendar is hung on the wall, you will lift the pages from the bottom to the top to change the months. Open up to the first page. On the bottom half, leave a two-inch border around the sides and bottom, and draw a rectangle using your ruler.

4 To make the grid for the calendar days, you will need seven equally sized boxes (seven days in a week) across and five of the same size boxes down (approximately five weeks in a month). Use your ruler to measure the boxes.

5 Above the boxes write the days of the week. Many calendars start with Sunday and go through Saturday, but you can make it start Monday and go through Sunday. If you want to get a little crazy, start your week with your favorite day!

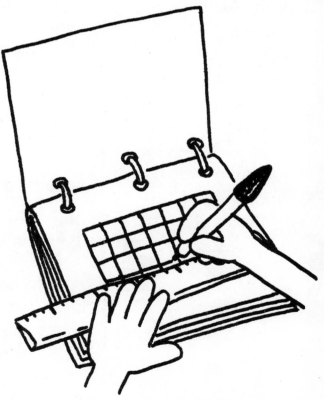

6 Once your grid is drawn, look at an upcoming calendar for the month you will start with. Write in the month at the top of the grid above the days of the week. Begin on the first day of the month with 1 and number each box with as many days as there are in the month. January, March, May, July, August, October, and December all have 31 days. April, June, September, and November have 30 days, and February has 28 or 29 days, depending on if it is a leap year. (Future leap years are 2000, 2004, and 2008 and contain 29 days in February.)

7 Draw a grid for all 12 months. Continue to check your days and dates against a calendar, since it is easy to confuse the days as you switch from month to month.

8 Glue the chosen photos at the top of each page for the corresponding months.

9 If you are giving this as a gift, write a personal note and sign the back page. You may even want to write in some important dates not to be forgotten, such as "First Day of School," "Lori's Birthday," or "Gram and Gramps come to town." Now your personalized calendar is ready to hang on the wall.

Fool your friends into thinking you were with Brad Pitt or Winona Ryder by inserting your face into an existing picture and hanging it on your wall! (It'll at least make them do a double take!)

MATERIALS

- celebrity magazine
- clear plastic box frame (5" x 7" works best)
- scissors
- glue

PHOTO PREP!

Choose a picture from the magazine that features at least two people, one of them being the person you want to be seen with. Make sure that it will fit into the size frame you have. Then find a picture of yourself in which your face is approximately the same size as the people in the photograph.

WHAT TO DO

1 Open the clear box frame and take out the paper that is inserted between the plastic and the cardboard box. Use this as a guide to cut out the right size picture from the magazine, then cut out the picture you have chosen.

2 Using the scissors, cut out the face of the person in the photo you want to replace. Start in the middle of the face with a small hole and carefully cut around the face. Try to make the cut as neat as possible.

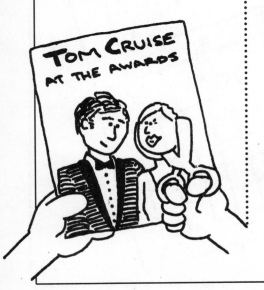

TOM CRUISE AT THE AWARDS

You may want to leave that person's hair and give yourself a new "do." Or, you can neatly trim away the person's hair and use your own pictured in your photo.

3 Use the face you cut out of the magazine as a guide to choosing the picture of yourself. The faces should be about the same size, but cut your picture larger than the size of the hole, so that you have room to glue it on the back. Insert your face on the back of the magazine, lining up your face so that it looks real. Let the glue dry completely.

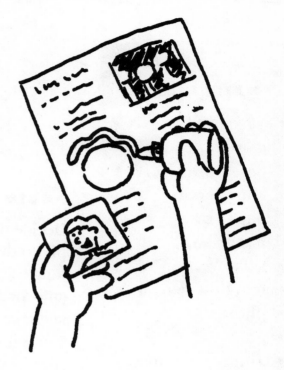

4 While the picture is drying, create a headline in bold letters, sure to draw attention—or at least a few laughs.

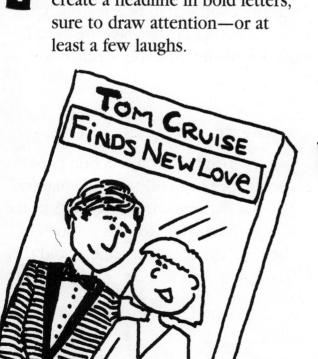

5 Put the new picture into the clear plastic frame, then place the headline above or below, wherever it fits best, and hang it on the wall. You are sure to impress your friends!

Breakfast of Champions

Impress your friends by offering them a breakfast cereal with your name and picture on it. Perfect for the morning after a sleep-over!

PHOTO PREP!

Decide on the theme of your cereal. Choose a photo that represents it well. Call it George of the Jungle and take a picture of yourself in a tree with an expedition hat on, or call it Beach Nut Bonanza and take a picture of yourself in beach attire. Or you can change the name of your favorite cereal, such as Wheaties to Peties, or Cap'n Crunch to Kristin Krunch.

MATERIALS

- 15-ounce cardboard cereal box
- construction paper or a paper bag
- scissors
- marking pens
- photos
- glue
- zipper lock bag
- raisins, oats, granola

WHAT TO DO

1 Get a cereal box, construction paper (or a paper bag), scissors, and markers. Cut out paper to cover the parts of the box you are going to change, such as the logo, the name, the photo, and the nutritional information.

2 To design your own cereal name, use big bubble lettering or script to write it. When you are finished, glue it onto the cereal box. Then glue your picture on the front of the box and decorate around it.

3 For the nutritional information on the side, include your age, height, weight, size, and so on. Get creative! The ingredients should include your hobbies and interests, such as: "great soccer skills, photographic eye, swimming, hiking, and killer volleyball serve."

4 You can use the real cereal that came in the box or make your own by combining raisins, oats, and granola in a gallon-size zipper lock bag to place inside the box. You are now ready to enjoy your Breakfast of Champions!

Personality Collage

Have a friend who needs his or her spirits lifted? Fill a frame with photos and cut out words that describe the friend's personality.

MATERIALS

- 5 to10 photos
- magazines
- scissors
- clear plastic frame (8" x 10" or 11" x 14")
- white glue

PHOTO PREP!

By combining words and photos to describe and represent your friend's personality, you can create a perfect personalized present! Pick 5 to 10 photos of him or her doing favorite activities or making silly faces, or choose a school picture.

WHAT TO DO

1 From the magazines, cut out positive and silly phrases and words that describe your friend. Look for specific captions for the photos you have chosen.

2 Open the plastic frame and take out the blank sheet of paper inside. Use this as your pasteup page. (If your frame doesn't contain a blank sheet, take a plain piece of paper and trim it to fit in the frame.)

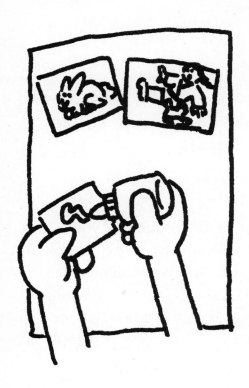

3 Arrange the pictures and the cutout words on the page, completely covering the paper. When you are happy with the layout, glue everything to the page. Let it dry completely.

4 Put it into the frame and, if you want, write the date on the back of the frame and sign your name. Give it to your friend who needs a smile. It is a gift that is sure to be treasured forever.

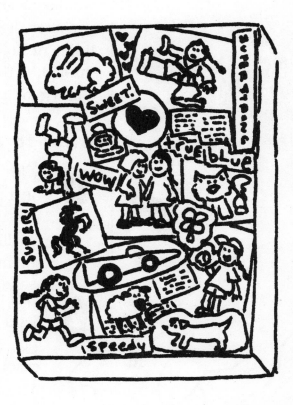

Photo Flip Book

Make a book of still photos that will appear like a movie scene when you flip through it.

PHOTO PREP!

All you need to prepare for this craft is your camera and a roll of film, at least 24 exposures. You will take a series of still photos of a subject that you alter slightly each time. When you assemble this series of photos together as a booklet and flip through it, the result will be pictures that look like a movie or a cartoon.

WHAT TO DO

1 With a piece of masking tape, mark a place on a table in a well-lit area. For this project, we suggest an apple that gets mysteriously smaller—one bite at a time! Set an apple on the mark and take one picture of it.

2 Pick up the apple and take a bite out of it. Set it back down on the masking tape mark. Take a picture of it while standing in the exact same spot as before. Alternate between bites of apple and taking pictures.

MATERIALS

- roll of film (24 exposures, 100 ASA)
- masking tape
- apple
- scissors
- thick construction paper
- large stapler
- marker

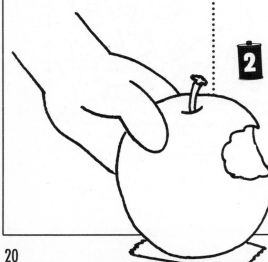

You will need to shoot a whole roll of 24 shots—one picture for each bite. The final picture should be the core of the apple.

3 Get your pictures developed. Request standard 3½" x 5" matte prints.

4 Keep the photos in the order that they were taken. You may want to lightly number each photo on the back.

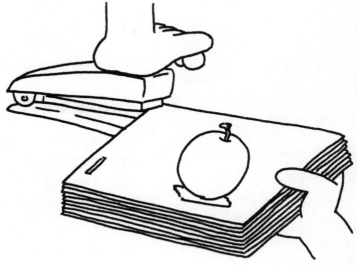

5 Cut two pieces of construction paper to the size of the photos. Place one on the front of the stack of photos and one on the back. Staple them all together on the left-hand side with a staple in each of the two corners.

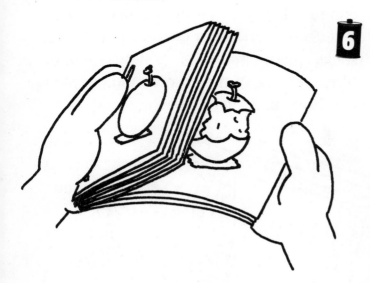

6 Give the book a title and write it in bold letters on the front cover. Now hold the book with your left hand and flip through the pages with your right hand to see the scene of the vanishing apple. You can create a Photo Flip Book with any image you choose! The secret is to show only one small change per photo.

Crafty Frame

Display your photos in this unique frame made from things you find or create yourself.

PHOTO PREP!

Pick a photo you want to display in your frame. Measure the size of the picture and make sure that the opening of the frame you make fits the size of the photo.

WHAT TO DO

 Line your work area with newspaper. Arrange the Popsicle sticks into a square and glue them together. Let them dry completely. If your photo is rectangular, you will need to arrange a couple of layers of sticks lengthwise to fit (see illustration). Overlap some of the corners and edges to reinforce the structure of the frame.

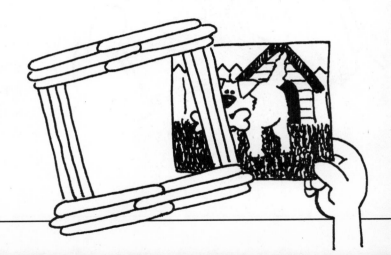

MATERIALS

- photograph
- newspaper
- Popsicle® sticks or twigs
- white glue
- craft glue for wood surfaces (optional)
- glue gun (with adult's help only)
- small decorative objects, such as beads, glitter, and lace
- scissors
- cardboard

2 To make a frame using twigs, arrange 4 to 12 twigs into a square or rectangular shape, overlapping the corners.

3 Glue the twigs together with white glue or a craft glue made especially for bonding wood surfaces.

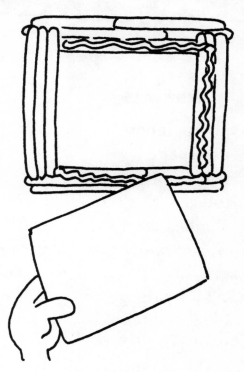

4 Choose a theme to decorate your frame. If your photo is a nature shot, you may want to glue little pine cones and dried flowers around the edges. Or you can use beads, glitter, or lace. Set your decorated frame aside to dry.

5 To make a backing for the frame, cut out a piece of cardboard that is a little larger than the size of the opening of the frame.

6 Glue down the backing on three sides only, for you need to leave an opening on the top or side to insert the photo. Let the glue dry, then insert your photo. Now you have a really neat frame!

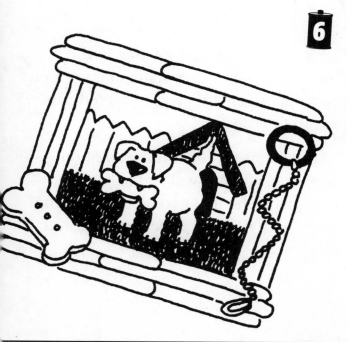

Creative Photo Candles

MATERIALS

- photographs
- newspaper
- two empty cans (bigger than the candles used)
- waxed paper
- scissors
- 2-inch tall (or bigger) thick white or off-white candles
- straight pins
- medium cooking pot
- 1 lb. of wax cut into small chunks
- tablespoon
- teaspoon
- stearin (found in art/craft stores)
- candy thermometer

Use your photos to make personalized photo candles. The candles burn, but the photos don't! They make great gifts!

PHOTO PREP!

Choose the photos you want to put on your candles. Make sure that the area of the picture you want to display fits on the candle you are using.

WHAT TO DO

1 Choose a work area near the stove and line it with newspaper. Fill one of the empty cans with warm water and set it on the work area. Put a sheet of waxed paper next to the can.

2 Using scissors, cut the photos to fit onto the size candle you will be using. The photograph should fit comfortably on the candle with no extra edges hanging over.

3 Roll the photo around the candle to help it take the form of the candle. Secure the photo in place using four straight pins. Set the candle on its side and push a pin in each corner of the photo. Make sure you push the pins in far enough so that the candle will fit inside the cans. The pins may not push in easily. If this is the case, get them started. Hold the candle gently and push the pin up against a hard surface (a door or a wall), and the pin should slide in with ease.

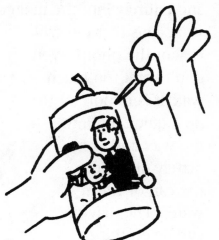

4 Fill a cooking pot half full with water. Place the second can in the pan of water and place the chunks of wax in the can. You don't want the wax to melt over the side of the can, so only melt what will fit in the can. As the first pieces melt, you will have room to add the additional wax until the whole pound is melted.

> You will need a parent or another adult to help you with the rest of the steps.

5 Turn the stove on to a very low heat and begin melting the wax chunks. Add 3 tablespoons of stearin to the melted wax. Continue adding wax to the can until it is deep enough to dip the entire candle you are using.

6 Make sure you keep the wax on low heat. Using a candy thermometer, keep the mixture at around 160 degrees during the dipping procedure. If it is too hot, the entire candle might melt—and if it is not hot enough, the layer of wax will be too thick and cloud the photographic image.

7 Holding the candle from the wick, dip it quickly and entirely into the melted wax. This first dip will mount the photo—you don't want too much wax. It is important to do a quick dip into the wax and immediately dip it into the can of warm water. Then lay the candle on the waxed paper.

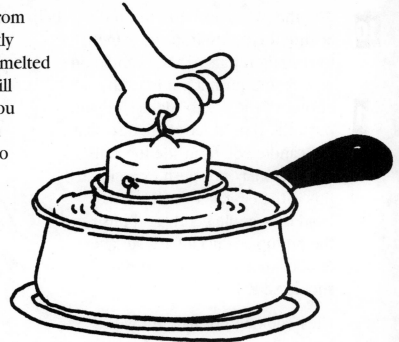

8 Remove the pins one at a time and gently roll the candle on the waxed paper to secure the photo. There will be small holes where you removed the pins. Carefully press on the area surrounding the holes to fill them in with wax. These holes will disappear in the next dipping step. The wax should not be hot at this point, but ask an adult to test it carefully.

9 Take the candle by the wick again and dip it quickly, first into the hot wax, then into the warm water and set it on the waxed paper. Flatten the bottom by pushing the candle down on the waxed paper. Be careful not to push too hard because the candle is still fragile and may collapse. Let it set on the waxed paper while you begin to dip your other prepared candles.

To make additional candles, follow steps 4 through 7, paying attention to the temperature of the melted wax.

 After you have dipped all your candles, add 1 teaspoon of stearin to the remaining wax and dip them all one more time. This will harden the candles and make them dripless.

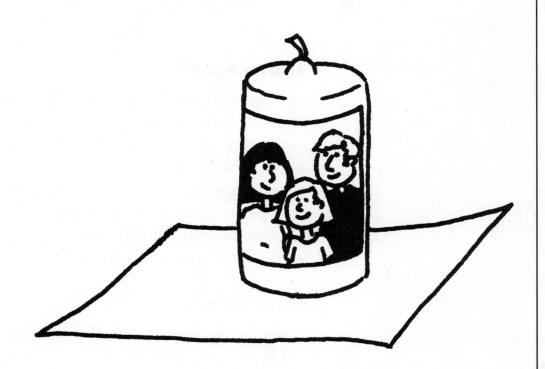

Photo Essay

Be a photojournalist! All you have to do is pick a subject and photograph it. Let the pictures tell the story. You can frame them or mount them in a series on foam board.

MATERIALS

- any 35mm camera
- 2 to 3 rolls of black-and-white or color film
- issues of *Life* magazine and *National Geographic*
- large sheet of foam board
- glue stick
- wall hanger

PHOTO PREP!

This craft focuses on telling a story through original pictures you take, called a photo essay. To prepare, find a camera you feel comfortable using, as well as two or three rolls of film. If you are trying to create a certain mood or tone with your photo essay, you may want to shoot with black-and-white film. Otherwise, color film works well in most situations.

WHAT TO DO

 Before you start to shoot any pictures, take time to look through a few issues of *Life* magazine and *National Geographic*. These two magazines use photojournalism to tell many of their stories. The job of a photo-journalist is to tell a story through a series of pictures.

Decide what type of photos you like best. Nature photography? Sports? People? Scenery? Travel? Think of a particular subject—a person, place, or an event—for your main focus. Now, what is the story you want to tell about your subject?

Maybe your subject is an athlete, and your focus is his or her training for an important match. Or perhaps you want to shoot a story on the new zoo in your area. You may want to focus in on the people behind the zoo, monkey faces, or a theme on a day at the zoo.

2 To figure out what kind of pictures would best tell the story, you need to create a shot list. A shot list is a list of images you will take to capture the story. It also helps you to organize your shooting schedule and gives you a checklist so that you do not forget anything. Remember that as you are shooting your story, you can add anything you want to the shot list.

Examples of what should be included in the shot lists:

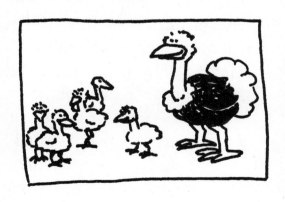

For an athlete—What parts of his or her day are devoted to training, preparing, and improving his or her sport? Take pictures of these things. For a place—What makes this place unique? Are there any landmarks or special views in this place that make it special? What do people do there? You should include all of these on your shot list. If you are creating "A Day in the Life," you should spend a whole day taking pictures of your subject.

You want to tell the whole story and represent the subject being featured in a series of 6 to 10 pictures.

3 Take the photos, and plan to use at least two to three rolls of film. For the final series, you will choose 6 to 10 pictures that tell the whole story, but you should shoot many pictures.

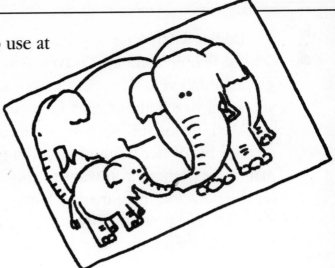

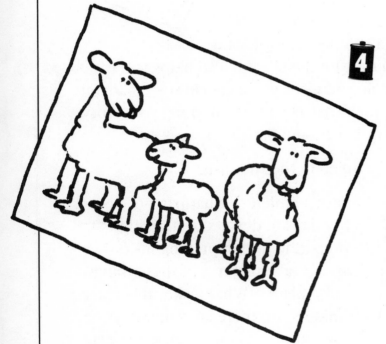

4 Have the pictures developed. You will edit, or choose, what pictures tell the story the best. This process usually starts with removing any pictures that are unclear or improperly exposed. Then if there are variations of the same picture, choose one or two that speak the most about the subject. Start to create a series of pictures that will best tell the story.

DID YOU KNOW?

A *National Geographic* photographer shoots approximately 200 rolls of film (that's over 7000 pictures!) per assignment. The final story will usually be a selection of 5 to 13 photos that best represent the subject.

5 Once you have chosen your photos, mount them on a large sheet of foam board. First arrange the photos as you want them to hang. Secure the pictures on the foam board with a glue stick. You can attach a wall hanger to the back of the foam board and hang it on the wall.

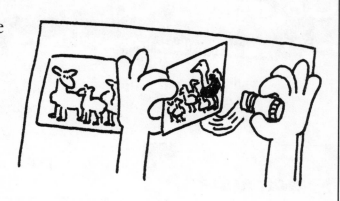

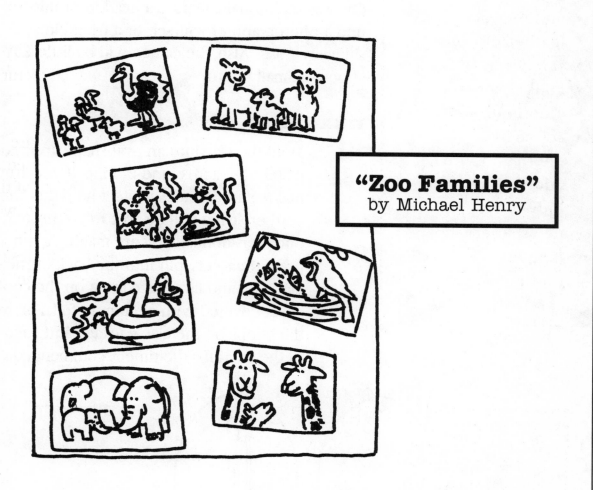

"Zoo Families"
by Michael Henry

Colorful Clay Cameo

Create a classic photographic cameo pin or necklace using a profile photo and clay.

PHOTO PREP!

Cameos traditionally feature a head in profile, so find a photograph of yourself or a friend in a sideview pose. Also, the cameo will be little, so choose a small photo.

WHAT TO DO

1. Mold the clay into an oval shape approximately 1½" across and 2" long. If you are making a necklace, create a hole that the cord or string will be able to go through once it is done. If you are making a pin, press the safety pin into the back of the clay oval and lay it facedown on the cookie sheet covered with aluminum foil. Follow directions on the clay package and bake it in the oven for the time recommended.

MATERIALS

- profile photo
- molding clay
- leather or cord
- safety pin
- cookie sheet
- aluminum foil
- scissors
- glue gun (with adult's help only)
- newspaper
- lacquer (optional)

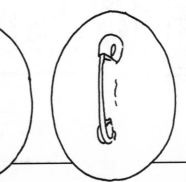

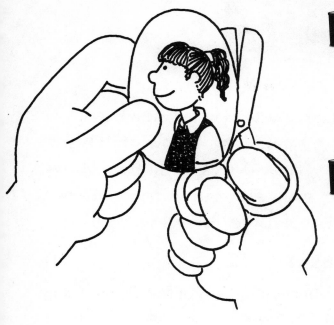

2 Let it cool completely. Now cut your picture to fit into the cameo shape. Have an adult help you use the hot glue gun to attach the photo to the cameo. Let it dry.

3 Lay the cameo on the newspaper and have an adult spray it with lacquer to seal it in and coat it. (This step is optional and should only be done with an adult's help.)

4 If it is going to be a necklace, thread the cord through the opening you made and tie it around your neck. If you decided to make it a pin, simply attach it with the safety pin onto your favorite blouse or jacket!

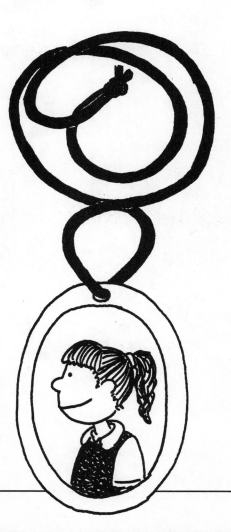

Funky Fridge Fotos

Create new family members using Mom's head, your brother's body, and Dad's legs! Turn them into magnets and display them on the fridge for all to see!

PHOTO PREP!

Find an assortment of photos of friends and family that you can cut up. Pictures should include full-body poses as well as close-ups.

WHAT TO DO

1 Lay out the photos that you want to cut and paste together. Choose a head for your newest family member, then carefully cut it out.

2 Carefully cut out the body you want to use so it matches up with the head. Finally, choose the legs and cut them out.

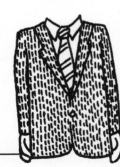

MATERIALS

- photographs of family and friends
- scissors
- thin cardboard
- Mod Podge™ (or other water based sealer, glue, and finish)
- glue
- magnet

3 Paste all the body parts together on a piece of thin cardboard using the Mod Podge. Let it dry completely. Carefully cut out your new person and turn it over.

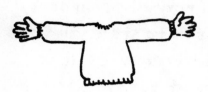

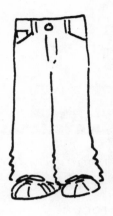

4 Use the glue to attach the magnet to the back of the person. Let this dry completely and then hang it on your fridge to hold important notes. Don't forget to name each new family member, too!

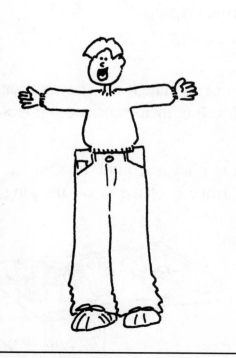

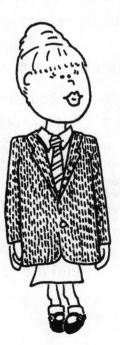

Memory Box

Instead of a normal scrapbook, create this box to store all your memories and treasures. It is especially great for three-dimensional mementos such as baseballs, autograph books, concert tickets, and so on.

MATERIALS

- photographs
- magazines
- recent newspapers
- sturdy shoe box
- mementos (movie tickets, stickers, notes, and so on)
- glue
- scissors
- glitter
- paintbrush
- Mod Podge™ (or other water based sealer, glue, and finish)
- puff pens

PHOTO PREP!

Gather pictures of yourself and your friends. Choose a variety of pictures, such as your school picture, family portraits, and fun photos of your pets. You can also cut out small pinups of your favorite celebrities from magazines.

WHAT TO DO

1. Clear a work area and line it with newspaper. Gather your shoe box, mementos, and supplies in the work area.

2. With glue, paste photos around the shoe box and lid. Create a collage by overlapping magazine cutouts, your mementos, and the photos.

Cut out part of a current newspaper that has the date on it and glue it on, too. If you want to decorate the box with glitter, just spread a dab of glue and sprinkle the glitter onto it. The glue will dry clear and the glitter will sparkle! Let the box dry completely.

3 Use the paintbrush to wipe a layer of Mod Podge over the entire box. Let this dry completely. With the puff pens, you can write your name and the year on the lid of the box.

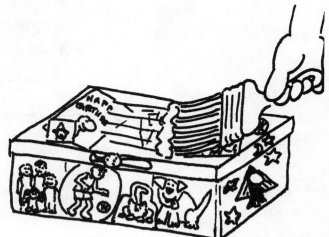

4 Once that is dry, put your treasures in the box and cover it with the lid. Now your memories will be safe and accessible for a long, long time. You may want to create a new memory box each year and keep the best items from that year in it.

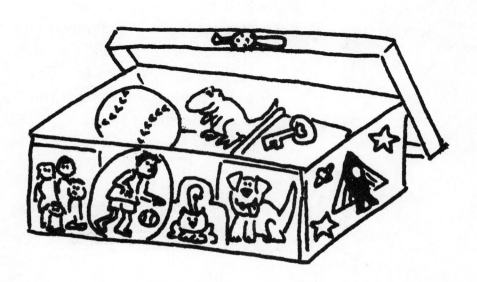

Mixed Tape Mania

There is no better treat than to compile a tape of your favorite songs and artists. Then complete the package by creating your own tape jacket.

MATERIALS

- cassette tape of your favorite songs
- cassette tape jacket
- plastic cassette container
- construction paper
- pen or pencil
- scissors
- glue
- ruler

PHOTO PREP!

Since a cassette tape holder is not very big, any photos you use in this will have to be small. Normal 3½" x 5" photos will work, but you need to trim down these pictures and spread them around so that you can feature more pictures on your cassette jacket.

WHAT TO DO

 First you want to record a tape full of your favorite tunes. Depending on the equipment you have, you can tape the music from the radio or from various CDs or tapes. Be sure to keep a list of the songs you tape. (You'll need it in step 4.)

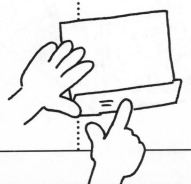

2 Remove the cardstock jacket from your plastic cassette container and lay it on the construction paper. Trace around it with a pen or pencil. Cut out the outline on the construction paper and crease it along the same folds as the original jacket.

3 Arrange your photos on the paper jacket. Be aware of the folds and try to place your photos around the folding areas. Glue your photos onto the cassette jacket.

4 On the back part of the jacket that you can see through the plastic, list the songs you have included on your tape. Inside the foldout jacket, you can also write any fun information about the songs. (The record industry calls these liner notes.)

5 Give the tape a title and write it on the jacket so that when you fold it and insert it into the plastic cover, it will read on the back binding (see how the title is written on your model cassette). You can even put a very small picture here.

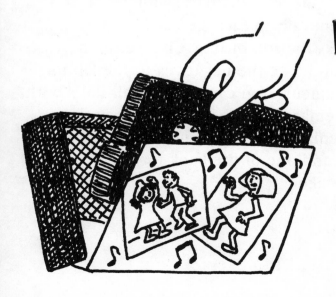

6 Insert your homemade tape jacket cover and tape into the plastic container. You now have a wonderful musical collection that can be listened to forever! (Well, maybe not forever, but it will be fun to pull out this tape in 10 years and hear the kind of music you used to love!)

Friendly Paper Dolls

Use photographs of your friends to make paper dolls, then cut out clothes from your favorite magazines with tabs so that you can dress the dolls.

MATERIALS

- any 35mm camera
- 8" x 10" photos of a friend, back and front
- thin cardboard
- Mod Podge™ (or other water based sealer, glue, and finish)
- scissors
- magazines
- pencil
- manila envelope

PHOTO PREP!

Set up your photo shoot outside in front of a neutral background such as a blank wall or a garage door. Have your friend put on a beige or black leotard or shorts and a tank top. Ask your friend to stand straight and still with arms down at his or her sides and legs slightly separated, looking straight on. Take some pictures from the front and some from the back, with the person posing identically in each.

Process the roll of film. Choose the best pictures and take the negatives to the lab for an enlargement. You can make small dolls with a 5" x 7" enlargement or larger ones with an 8" x 10" enlargement. You need one picture of the front and one of the back for each doll you want to make.

WHAT TO DO

1 Paste the front-side enlargement on a thin piece of cardboard using Mod Podge or another similar glue. Also, cover the entire photo with the Mod Podge. Let it dry completely.

2 Carefully cut out the perimeter of the doll following its outlines. Line up the back-side enlargement and cut it out to fit on the back of the cardboard doll.

3 Paste the back-side photo to the back of the doll using the Mod Podge. Let it dry completely. Trim any uneven edges. Seal up the sides of the doll using the Mod Podge around the edges. Hold the doll while it is drying so that it does not stick to anything.

4 To make the clothing and accessories, cut out pictures of your favorite clothes from a magazine and paste them onto thin cardboard. Make sure they are the right size to fit on the doll. Let them dry completely. Cut out hats, shoes, bags, purses, and other accessories, and glue them to the cardboard as well.

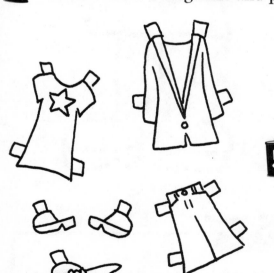

5 Before you cut the clothes and accessories from the cardboard, sketch in small tabs to hold everything in place on the doll. With a pencil, outline small tabs about ¼" square to hold the accessories on the doll. Make them on the top and bottom, and if it is a big item such as a jacket or a dress, you need to add some tabs to the sides.

Cut out the clothes and tabs. To dress your paper doll, fold the tabs around it to hang the clothes on it.

6 Find an envelope to store all of your clothes and accessories for each doll. A manila envelope works well. Write the name of the doll on the envelope. This personalized paper doll makes a great gift for a birthday girl or boy.

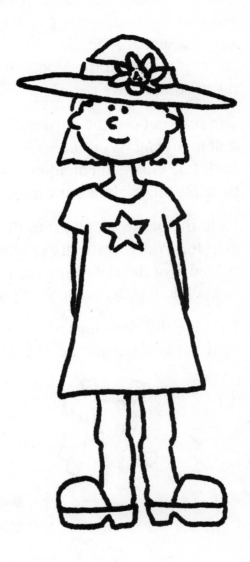

REMINDER

Never touch the negatives with your hands—any slight touch could scratch the negative or leave fingerprints. If your negatives are not in a plastic sleeve, only handle them from the outside edge of the serrated film.

Special Effects

Write your name with a flashlight for a ghostly effect and create a really impressive photograph that you can hang on your bedroom door!

PHOTO PREP!

There are three settings on the manual camera that you will control: the ASA, or film speed; the aperture, or f-stop; and the shutter speed.

The ASA window is found on the top of the camera. The speed of the film or ASA is found on the roll of film and should be set in the ASA window by rotating the dial to the appropriate setting. Typical ASA speeds are 100 and 400. For this craft, you will be using 400 speed, the best film for low light situations.

The aperture, or f-stop, controls the size of the opening in the lens. This setting is found on the lens and ranges from 2 to 22 depending on the lens. Here, the camera should be set to the widest opening, which is the smallest number available (2, 2.8, or 3.5).

The shutter speed controls how quickly the camera takes the picture once the button is pushed. The normal range of shutter speeds are from B (bulb) to 1000.

For Special Effects, use the B (bulb) setting, which allows you to hold the camera open for as long as you want to.

WHAT TO DO

1 For this project, while you work the camera, you will need a helper to operate the flashlight. Set the camera on the tripod.

2 On butcher paper, write your name in script using a thick black marker. Turn the paper over and outline the reverse script of your name with the black marker. Tape the paper—with your name reading backward—on the wall behind where the camera is set up.

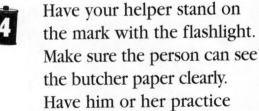

3 Look through the viewfinder and find the middle of the frame. Mark this spot on the floor—15 feet from the paper—with tape.

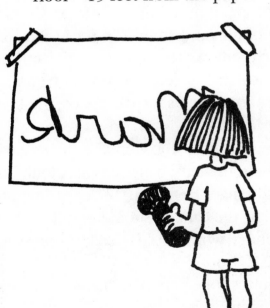

4 Have your helper stand on the mark with the flashlight. Make sure the person can see the butcher paper clearly. Have him or her practice outlining your name while standing on the mark.

5 Darken the room by closing all curtains and turning off all light sources.

6 You are now ready to begin taking pictures. Stand about 3 feet from the flashlight helper, facing him or her. Be sure to be out of the path between the flashlight and the butcher paper. Call "action" as you push down on the bulb setting. Keep the button pressed while your friend turns on the flashlight and outlines your name. (In the photo it will read correctly!)

7 Once the helper is done, he or she should turn off the flashlight. Then you must let go of the B setting. Wind the camera and start over, this time using your friend's name. You may want to take several pictures to ensure that one turns out the way you want.

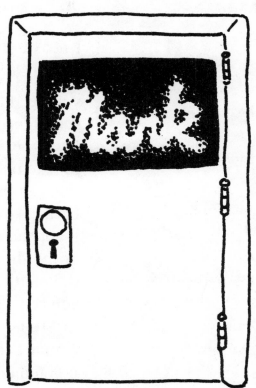

8 When you are done with the roll of film, have it processed at the lab and have prints made. This impressive photo—especially when enlarged!—makes a great nameplate on your bedroom door.

HOW THIS CRAFT WORKS

When the bulb setting is pressed, the camera is reading whatever light source is available. In the total darkness, it is blank. As you turn on the flashlight and use it as the light source, it is like painting light onto the negative.

Pleasing Pet Pictures

MATERIALS

- your pet
- large solid color sheet, such as dark gray, white, or black
- clothespins
- 2 to 3 clamp lights (basic lightbulb lights that have a clamp with a small metal reflector, found at any hardware store)
- props, such as funny hats or sunglasses
- film
- any 35mm camera
- pet treats
- frame (optional)

Take portraits of your pet the pros will admire!

PHOTO PREP!

To take professional-looking portraits of your pet, you need to set up your own studio. This involves setting up a backdrop and lighting the area with a few basic light sources. Pick where you are going to take the portraits and set up your backdrop. You can use clothespins and attach it to the curtains in your bedroom or living room. Attach it approximately 4 feet high and spread the rest of the sheet on the floor so that when you take the picture, the sheet will be the only background you see.

To light your "studio," arrange the clamp lights around the room. You need one main light that is pointed directly at your pet. The other one or two lights will be used as "fill" lights—point one at the backdrop sheet and one at the back of your pet. Clamp the lights directly onto the back of a chair. This will fill in shadows that may be cast from your main light source. Once you put your pet in place, you might want to change the lights a little for effect.

WHAT TO DO

1 Gather and arrange any props you will be using. Make sure you have film in your camera and that once you pose your pet you are ready to take the pictures.

2 Put your pet in place and quickly dress it in its costume. Rearrange the lights, trying to conceal any harsh shadows.

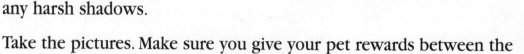

3 Take the pictures. Make sure you give your pet rewards between the shots! Have the film processed at a local lab.

4 Choose your favorite picture and place it in a simple frame. You may even want to blow it up to poster size to hang on your wall or to give to your favorite animal lover.

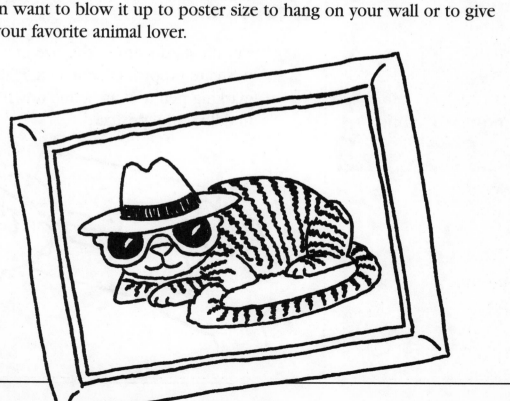

Photo Postcards

Make photo postcards that you can send through the mail using your favorite photos. Perfect for long-distance relationships.

PHOTO PREP!

Choose a favorite picture of yourself to send to your grandparents. Or send a nice portrait of your dog to a friend who just moved. The photos should be 3½" x 5" and can be color or black-and-white.

WHAT TO DO

1 Cut the cardboard to the size of a normal postcard (approximately 3" x 5"). Use a marking pen to draw a line down the middle of the postcard.

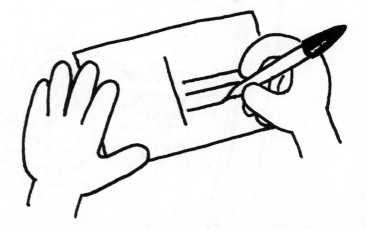

MATERIALS

- photographs
- scissors
- cardboard
- marker
- pen
- glue
- glitter
- postcard stamp

2 With a pen, write your note on the left side of the postcard and fill in the address of the person you are sending it to on the lower right side.

3 Glue your photo to the other side of the card. Decorate the photo with clever sayings from magazines or with glitter. Let the glue dry completely.

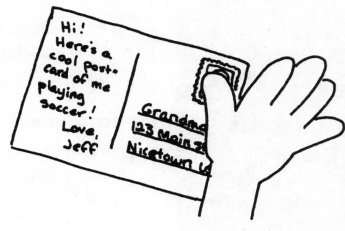

4 Turn the card over and place the stamp in the upper right-hand corner. Make sure you use a postcard stamp or equivalent postage.

5 Finally, drop the card in the mailbox and enjoy the happy response of the person who received your personal card.

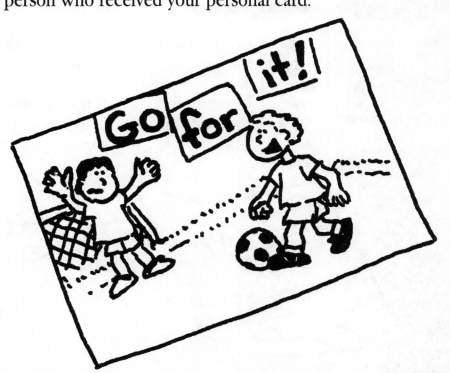

Photo Puzzle

Create your own puzzle using your favorite pictures. Challenge a friend to assemble your puzzle.

PHOTO PREP!

Take your favorite picture and have a color photocopy made of it. At the same time, enlarge the photo to 5" x 7" or 8" x 10". You can have this whole process done at any office center. This way, you won't destroy the original photo, and it can be enlarged to the exact puzzle size you want.

WHAT TO DO

1 Lay newspaper around your work area. Gather all necessary supplies.

2 Using Mod Podge, affix your photocopy to the cardboard. Then cover the photo completely with the Mod Podge. Let it dry.

MATERIALS

- photographs
- newspaper
- Mod Podge™ (or other water based sealer, glue, and finish)
- thin cardboard
- scissors
- envelope

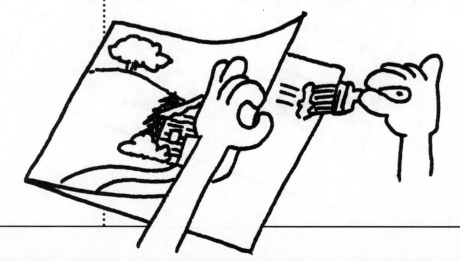

3 Carefully cut out shapes using scissors. You can cut typical shapes that resemble other puzzle pieces or you can make up your own. If you are creating your own shapes, make sure to cut pieces that will attach to one another.

4 Place the puzzle pieces in an envelope with a clasp to keep from losing any of the pieces. If you are giving it to someone as a gift, take the pieces apart before putting the puzzle into the envelope.

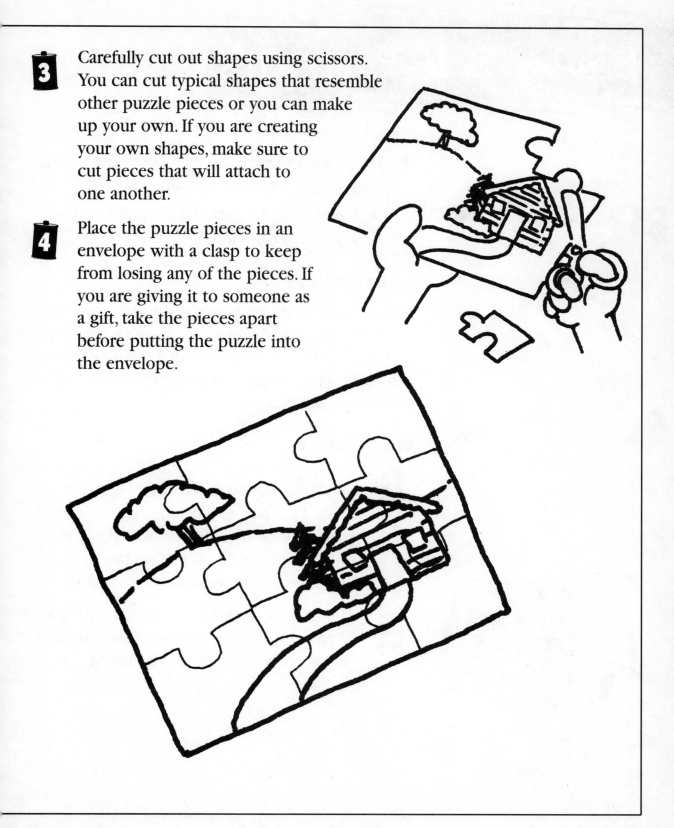

Savvy Self-Portraits

Using the timer on your camera, take pictures of yourself. Try to capture different aspects of your personality.

MATERIALS

- camera with a self-timer
- film
- tripod
- poster board
- glue

PHOTO PREP!

Decide what kind of pictures you want to take of yourself. You can take funny pictures or serious pictures. You can also take several pictures that represent different parts of your personality or show what hobbies you like.

WHAT TO DO

1 Set up your tripod on a flat surface. Open it up all the way so that it stands steady. Extend the legs to a height that will allow you to see through the camera. If you do not have a tripod, you can set the camera on a steady counter, a table, or a ledge.

2 Mount the camera on the tripod. There is usually a screw on the mounting plate that goes into the bottom of the camera.

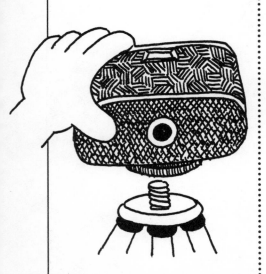

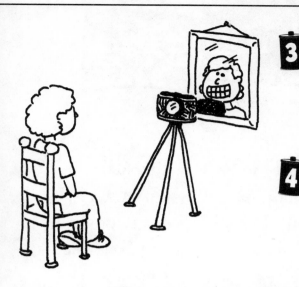

3 Decide where you want to pose and focus the camera on that place. If you want to see what you look like, place a mirror directly behind the camera pointed toward you.

4 Once you are ready to photograph "your subject," push the automatic timer and run into place. Most self-timers give you approximately 10 seconds before they trigger. The flashing red timer light will usually start moving really fast just before the camera is about to go off.

5 Take several variations of pictures. Remember, if you move the camera at all and you are using manual focus, you have to refocus the camera on the place where you'll be posing.

6 Have your pictures developed and arrange your photos on a poster board. Glue them in place. This is a great way to display your many talents, and it also makes a wonderful gift for proud parents and grandparents!

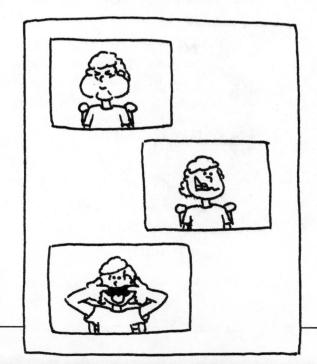

Wrap-It-Up Wall Hanging

Do away with traditional wrapping paper! Instead, wrap a present for your friend in plain paper and use photographs to decorate and personalize the wrapping. It will be such a masterpiece, your friend will want to hang it on the wall!

MATERIALS

- 3 to 10 photographs
- box to put present in (if gift is not already square and/or flat)
- paper shopping bag
- scissors
- white glue
- two sticks or two small tree branches
- twine or ribbon
- stapler
- tape

PHOTO PREP!

Choose the photos you want to include on the package. You may want to cut the photos, use whole photos, or use a combination of the two.

WHAT TO DO

1 For a simpler time wrapping, put your present into a square or rectangular box.

2 Take the paper bag and, using scissors, cut along the edge of one side until you get to the bottom of the bag. Cut out the bottom of the bag by following the seam all the way around until you have a flat piece of brown paper.

3 Lay the plain side of the paper facedown (you want the plain side to show), and place your present in the middle of the paper. Wrap the gift. You may want to get a parent or an older brother or sister to help you wrap it neatly.

4 Arrange the photographs on the package and glue them in place. Remember, you can put them all over the package. Once your friend has opened the package, he or she will be able to hang the wrapping paper on the wall. Include sticks or natural branches as part of the bow, and your friend can hang the paper from the branches as a wall hanging.

5 To make the wall hanging sticks, measure the length of the package. Find a twig or a branch that is a little bigger than the length of the paper.

6 Tie the sticks into the twine or the ribbon with a little instruction booklet that will tell your friend how to assemble the wall hanging. The instructions should read something like this:

This very special wrapping paper can be made into a wall hanging that you can keep forever. Open the package carefully. (If you lay the paper facedown, you can iron out any folds in the paper by using an iron—but only with an adult's help!)

Take a stick and carefully fold the top of the paper around it. Do the same on the bottom. Use a stapler to staple the sticks in place. Now cut pieces of the ribbon from the package and tie them onto each end of the stick. Your wrapping paper can now be displayed on the wall.

7 To address the package, you can make a gift card and write "To:" and put a photo of the person you are giving the present to, and "From:" with a photo of yourself! Have fun and be creative!

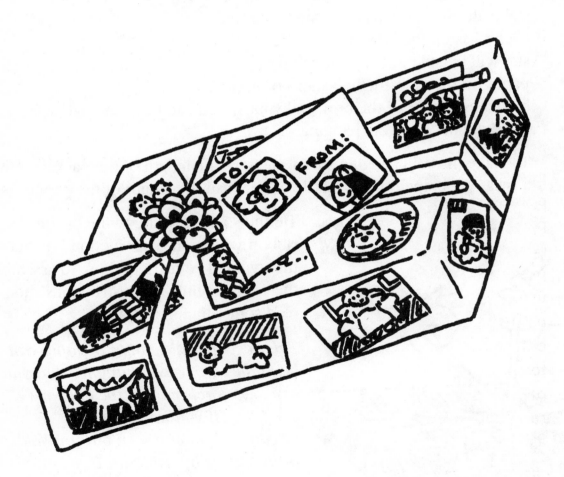

Color Your Memories

Create those artistic images you see on cards and calendars using your own black-and-white photographs.

MATERIALS

- black-and-white photographs (8" x 10" or bigger)
- newspaper
- cotton balls
- PM solution (to dilute the paints)
- photo oil paints
- paint palette (any wood or plastic surface used to mix paints)
- cotton swabs
- towel
- photo paint remover, such as Marlene's

PHOTO PREP!

Choose the photographs you want to tint. Enlargements of 8" x 10" or bigger are easiest to learn with because the areas you want to tint will be larger. However, any size black-and-white photograph can be used. Please note: the paint materials for this craft are more expensive than others in this book. Be sure to get a parent's permission before buying any materials.

WHAT TO DO

1 Line your work area with newspaper. Arrange the photographs you are going to paint on. You might want to first practice on pictures that you have many copies of.

2 Using the cotton balls, rub a layer of the PM solution over the entire photograph. Let it dry for a minute and then rub over it with a clean cotton ball.

3 Choose an area in the middle of the photograph at which to begin (usually the face of a person or the center of the image), and work toward the edge.

4 Put a small amount of paint (less than the size of a dime) onto the paint palette. A little bit goes a long way. You can mix your colors by blending two or three of them to get the colors you want.

5 Using a cotton swab, dab a little bit of paint and blot onto a towel. Make sure you use a different cotton swab for each color or combination of colors. Choosing the colors to paint with is easy. Usually, the photo paint colors are identified as cheeks, eyes, lips, and so on.

6 In small circular motions, apply the paint to the area in which you are working. Continue doing this until you achieve the desired color. If you make a mistake or go outside the lines, do not worry about it. Paint remover will be used to correct any mistakes after you are done.

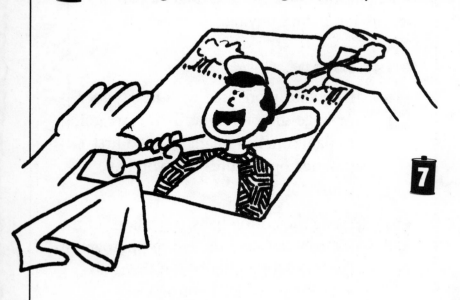

7 When you have completed painting the photograph, rub over the entire piece with a clean cotton ball. This will blend the colors and smooth out the surface.

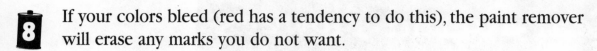 If your colors bleed (red has a tendency to do this), the paint remover will erase any marks you do not want.

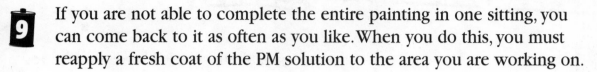 If you are not able to complete the entire painting in one sitting, you can come back to it as often as you like. When you do this, you must reapply a fresh coat of the PM solution to the area you are working on.

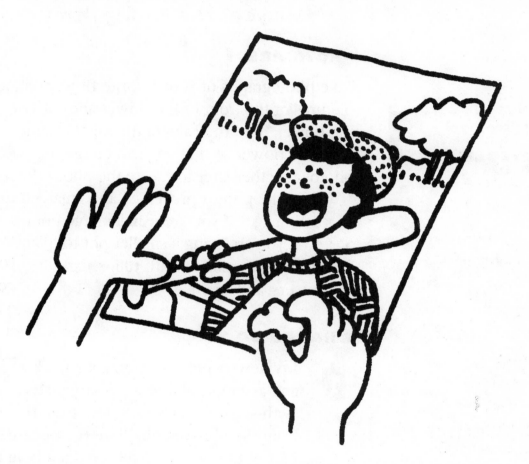

REMEMBER

The use of color on black-and-white photographs should be used for dramatic effect. Carefully choose the areas you want to highlight and have fun experimenting and creating memorable images!

Year-Round Flowers

Make a flowerpot that will bloom all year round using photographs!

PHOTO PREP!

Take photographs of your favorite flowers. Shoot pictures of the front of the flower and the back of the flower. Hold the camera the same distance from the flower so that you can merge the two photos together later to create the photo flower.

Have the photos processed and enlarged to 8" x 10" images if you are using a large pot or 5" x 7" if you are using a smaller pot to "plant" your flowers in. Experiment with tulips, daffodils, sunflowers, and so on.

WHAT TO DO

1 Lay newspaper down on your work area and assemble all the necessary materials. With scissors, carefully cut out the flowers from the photographs. Save the discarded part of the photos to fill the drain hole of the pot in step 5.

2 Using a ruler, measure the length of the full flower plus the depth of the clay pot. Cut the wire or coat hanger to this length using wire cutters, with an adult's help.

MATERIALS

- any 35mm camera
- color film
- terra-cotta clay pot
- newspaper
- scissors
- ruler
- stiff wire or coat hanger
- wire cutters
- glue
- dirt

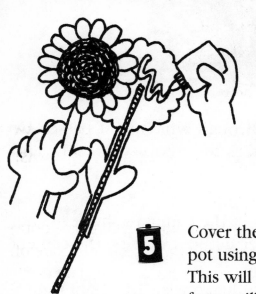

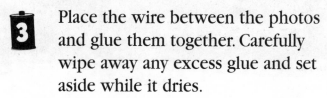

3 Place the wire between the photos and glue them together. Carefully wipe away any excess glue and set aside while it dries.

4 Prepare 3 to 5 photo flowers for your pot following steps 1 through 3.

5 Cover the drain hole of the clay pot using the excess photographs. This will prevent the dirt from spilling whenever the flowerpot is moved.

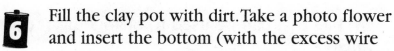

6 Fill the clay pot with dirt. Take a photo flower and insert the bottom (with the excess wire hanging out) into the dirt. Arrange the additional photo flowers in the pot as you want them. Secure them by packing the dirt firmly to hold the wire in place. If needed, add a little more dirt. Make sure that the stem of each photo flower is buried in the dirt. Enjoy!

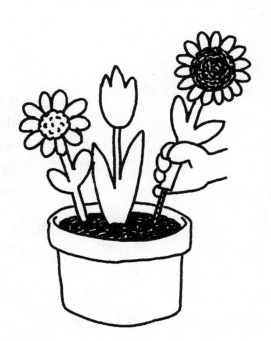

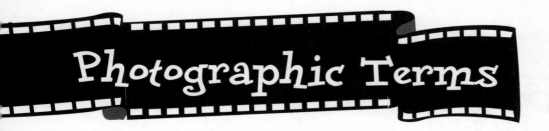

Aperture: The size of the lens opening through which light passes. On the camera this measurement is expressed as the f-stop—f/16, f/11, and so on.

Cable Release: A long wire that attaches to the camera's shutter release. This allows you to push the shutter without moving the camera.

Camera: A picture-taking device that usually consists of a light-tight box, a film holder, a shutter to admit a measured quantity of light, and a lens to focus the image.

Changing Bag: A light-tight bag that can be used to change film when a darkroom is not available.

Chrome: Color transparency or slide.

Crop: To trim the edges or narrow in on a specific area that will improve the composition.

Darkroom: A light-tight room where photographs are developed and printed.

Depth of Field: The amount of space that the camera can take a clear picture of. The depth of field can be controlled by the length of the lens, the aperture, and the distance from the subject.

Enlarger: An optical instrument used to project an image of a negative onto photographic paper to create a photograph.

Exposure: The amount of light that reaches the film.

Film: The light-sensitive material used in a camera to record a photographic image.

Film Speed: The relative sensitivity to light. These are recorded as ISO or ASA speeds. The slower films such as 50 ASA or 100 ASA will provide the clearest image with the most detail, while the faster films such as 400 ASA or 800 ASA will capture movement and work well in low light situations.

Filter: A piece of colored glass, plastic, or other material that will absorb some of the light rays going into the camera.

Fixer: A chemical solution that makes the photograph no longer sensitive to light. It seals the image.

Flash: A light source that emits a brief burst of light on a subject.

Lens: A piece or several pieces of optical glass shaped to focus an image of a subject.

Mod Podge™: This sealer-glue-finish wrapped into one will attach your photos to cardboard and also leave a clear flat finish that protects the photos. It is nontoxic and nonflammable, but once it dries it will not come off. If it is spilled on something, wipe it up immediately with water.

Negative: Black-and-white or color print film that makes tones opposite to what they really are. This is then projected onto paper to make a photographic print.

Print: A photograph.

Proof Sheet: Also called a contact sheet, it is a page of the negatives in full frame on photographic paper. This is useful in editing.

Push: To expose film at a higher film speed rating than normal.

Safelight: A light used in the darkroom during printing that will not expose the photographic paper.

Shutter: A mechanism that opens and closes to admit light into a camera for a measured length of time.

Slide: A transparency or a positive image that is mounted in a cardboard or glass mount.

Tank: A container that is light-tight used for developing film.

Tear Sheets: The term is for copies of publications in which a photographer's pictures appeared. These are usually kept in a portfolio.

Tripod: A three-legged support for a camera that is adjustable and steady. A monopod has only one leg and is useful for helping to steady the camera.